990

name : Jennifer Nellist
age: 12
address: 28, Glamis Gdns, [...]
    SCOTLAND UK EUROPE
fav animal : equine   (horse, pony, donkey, mule,
                    Jennet + zebra)

fav mag : PONY
fav food: Haggis
fav pony: Toro + Winnie + Leprecorn

Show Pony

An Illustrated
Teach Yourself book

Judging at the Greater London Horse Show

Jennifer and
Dorian Williams

Illustrated Teach Yourself **Show Pony**

with chapter heads by
Thelwell
diagrams by
Nancy Ablett

TREASURE PRESS

a beautifully turned
out pony and rider

Contents

First published in Great Britain in 1961 by Brockhampton Press
(now Hodder & Stoughton Children's Books)

This edition published in 1984 by
Treasure Press
59 Grosvenor Street
London W1

ISBN 0 907812 72 4

Printed in Hong Kong

Black and white photographs by Jamie Hodgson
Photograph of mounted policeman on page 24 by
courtesy of *British Travel Association*
Frontispiece photograph by Tony Stone Associates/Sue Streeter

Colour photographs
by John Nestle

1 Introduction

It is surprising but true that there are over two
thousand horse shows held each year in Britain
between the end of March and the beginning of
October. They range from the Royal Inter-
national Horse Show at the White City and the
Horse of the Year Show at Wembley to gymkhanas and church fêtes where a leading rein
class is included as an attraction. It would be
impossible to guess just how many ponies and
riders take part in all these shows, but one would
be safe to say that only a fraction of them really
do justice to themselves. Like everything else,
there is much more to it than meets the eye, and
so few of all the children that ride in shows
realize how much they themselves can do to give
themselves a better chance. Properly shown, a
quite moderate pony can win a lot of prizes : the
best-looking pony in the world will be overlooked

by the judges if the best in it is not brought out.

In the whole of Britain, although the standard of ponies is so wonderfully high – far higher than anywhere else in the world – there are probably a mere handful of ponies that can be labelled as absolutely top-class. But there are still all these hundreds of prizes to be won all over Britain each year : prizes even easier to win by the fact that at the majority of shows the pony classes are divided into different heights – 14·2 hands and under, 13·2 hands under, 12·2 hands under, and leading rein. Some shows even have classes for local children, or special breeds, or novice ponies and riders. And sometimes there are even consolation classes as well.

So do not be so despondent because your pony does not look like another 'Mr Crisp' or 'Pretty Polly' or 'Arden Bronze'. Very few do. You can still have great fun and win lots of rosettes in the show ring if you will take a little trouble.

More than that, all your efforts, all the hard work you put in will teach you a great deal that you will find extremely useful in other forms of riding, whether it's hunting or gymkhanas or just hacking. All that you have learnt about looking after and grooming your pony for the show ring will enable you to have a pony for ordinary riding that will be the envy and admiration of all your friends, because he looks so smart and well turned out. All that you have learnt about cleaning tack will mean that your equipment will last much longer because it is properly looked after. All that you have learnt about schooling and riding your pony properly – as you must, of course, in the show ring world – will mean that you have a good seat, with your legs in the proper position, your balance correct and your seat independent of your hands; and it will mean, too, that you have good hands so that other ponies, and horses when you are old enough to ride them, will go well for you – and it is not many people for whom strange horses and ponies do go well. And all that you have learnt about dressing yourself properly and being well turned out will mean that you will always look smart. That suggests that you are proficient and capable as a rider, and may very easily mean that some-body will notice you and invite you to ride for them.

You will have learnt too, by getting a pony into show condition, a great deal about horse-manship – not only feeding and working, but about conformation and ailments as well. You will have learnt to notice when a pony's legs are filled, when he is not sound, when he has a curb or a bad splint or some other unsoundness

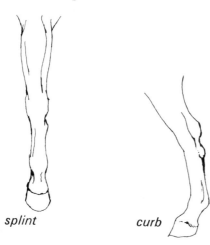

splint   curb

that will mean his being turned down by a judge. All this will be of the greatest use to you when you are old enough to be choosing a pony or horse for yourself. It is all too easy to be caught out and spend far more on a horse or pony than he is really worth, because of some unsoundness which a less experienced person will miss.

But best of all, perhaps, you will have had a great deal of fun from showing. It is always good fun to compete against other people and, win or lose, you learn a lot, enjoy yourself a lot, and indirectly do a great deal to help the survival of horses and ponies by drawing people's attention to their existence.

Win or lose! If you are going to resent losing then it is much better that you should not take up showing at all. Judges are bound to have different opinions. Ponies are bound to be better some days than others. Certain types of rings – too big or too small, full of jumps, or being in the middle of a fairground – will suit some ponies better than others. So no one has an undisputed *right* to win. It is for the judges to decide, and they will judge *on the day*. Even if your pony which won at the White City last week only comes out of the ring with a green or a yellow rosette, *smile*. Don't blame the judges or run down your opponents: smile, be pleased for the riders who were lucky enough to be above you – and then see if you can think of any way in which your pony did not go as well as it should have done: any way in which you or your pony can improve.

The show ring – or collecting ring – is no

Angela Wells riding 'Bobby Boy', an ideal child's pony

place for temperament, and unfortunately there is far too much of it.

Showing can be great fun, because apart from the honour of winning a prize, there is all the excitement of going to a show, and taking a pony into the ring. It is the climax of a lot of hard work and preparation.

In fact the actual taking of your pony into a show ring is like the iceberg, which has far more below the surface of the sea than can be seen above it.

In the following chapters we are going to try to take you step by step from the day when you first get your pony, through all the hard work of schooling, training, grooming, kit-cleaning, preparation – right up to the day you file in, very smart and excited, one behind another from the collecting ring into the show ring before the critical, interested, watchful eyes of the judges.

2 The right sort of pony

Show ponies are expensive, especially those that
have already won; but it is really much more
fun if you can find your own pony that has not
been shown before, even if you only come third
or fourth or fifth. If you have really done it yourself you will get far more satisfaction and much
more of a thrill out of showing. People who have
paid a lot of money for their ponies feel they
must win and are disappointed if they don't,
whereas starting from nothing you have it all
before you.

In this short chapter we are going to tell you
a little of what to look for when you set off to
buy a pony.

The first important point to remember is that your pony is what *you* make it. Often people think a pony that is first-class when they buy it will continue to be first-class with its new owner. But no, not always, by any means: a moderate or inexperienced rider can soon ruin a pony. On the other hand, if you are prepared to work really hard along the lines suggested in the next few chapters, you can turn quite an ordinary pony into a good one. Not an absolutely top-class one perhaps, that will win at the White City or Wembley, but one on which you will do very well. Obviously, though, it must be basically right.

Looking at a horse or pony is always a matter of being knowledgeable about its finer points, so if you set off to buy a pony it is as well to have someone experienced with you.

a common head   *a quality head*

Head A pony that is going to look attractive in the ring needs a small, pretty head, with a happy, bright expression. A large head and a Roman nose is never very nice. Nor lop ears. Ears have so much to do with expression. Large ears are never as flattering as small ones.

A kind eye means a great deal as far as temperament is concerned. Avoid a wild eye, or indeed any pony that appears to be vicious.

The front

The front of the pony should be deep with a long, sloping shoulder and a good-shaped neck. A 'loaded' shoulder, that is one that is all roly-poly, is always ugly, and a pony with a neck that seems upside-down will never get far.

A good front is always important in conformation, because a pony with a bad front – straight and narrow – is more difficult to school, being unable to move properly. It is much nicer riding a pony with a good front and plenty of length of rein. You feel more secure. On a pony with a bad front you feel as though you are sitting on a precipice.

A 'loaded' shoulder can be avoided up to a point by not letting a pony get too fat.

The neck should be swan-like. A 'U' neck has all the muscles developed underneath and none on top; whereas it is the top muscles that give a pony's neck shape. The neck can be improved by schooling, but bad hands will always make a pony stick his head up and his nose out, and this develops the under muscles.

The middle

A good-looking horse or pony always has a short back rather than a long one, with a good rib-cage. When you hear a judge say that a pony could do with another rib, it implies that the pony is long in the back. Always see that a pony

a rough pony before being prepared for the show ring

has plenty of heart room: that is, depth through the girth. A pony that is very shallow here is seldom elegant, and it often means that he is very narrow so that his front legs appear to come out of one hole.

The quarters   Good quarters – in show condition they will be

fat and rounded – always look a real part of the horse. They must not trail away. Nor do they want to slope too steeply. From behind they want to look level and square. There must not be a gap where the loins are, or you can be sure that you are going to have a job keeping the pony 'made up': he will always look in two parts.

the well-turned-out pony – a nice little show bridle with stitched nose-band and coloured brow band – a narrow webbing girth looks neat; a straight cut saddle shows off the pony's shoulders – some judges would prefer two or three fewer plaits

17

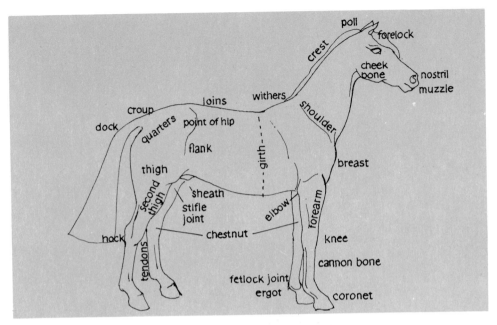

The tail

A tail that is set on high and well carried always gives a pony more presence than one that is set on low and droops. A great deal, of course, can be done with the actual shape of the tail, as long as it is well set on, as we shall be telling you later.

The hind-leg

A weak hind-leg can completely spoil the action of a pony, as that is where its impulsion comes from.

Looking at the hind-legs from behind be sure that the hocks are not too close and that the pony does not turn his feet out. That is a sure sign of weakness. If hocks are too close together they are called 'cow-hocks'. A pony with a weak hind-leg will often damage himself by knocking one leg with the other, especially the fetlock joint. This is called brushing.

strong hind legs

18

Always look at a pony's feet. Half the trouble with ponies' legs stems from bad feet. They should not be cracked or brittle or have rings round them.

Feet

bad

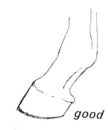

good

See that a pony stands well and square on all four legs; observe carefully the proportion of the leg to the body. A pony with long legs often has a shallow girth. Feel the bone. It is the bone beneath the knee that takes the strain; therefore a pony needs plenty of bone here. Puffy-looking legs mean wind-galls, and this suggests that the pony has already done a lot of work and might not stand much more.

Legs

A splint is a slight detriment to a show pony, though a veterinary surgeon can give you something to help get rid of it. For other unsoundness, such as curbs, we suggest you ask your vet, or read it up in a book. There are plenty of good, simple books on ailments.

The front leg wants to be straight with a short cannon-bone and a pastern not too long and sloping. A pony should neither be over at the knee nor back at the knee. Nor should he give the impression of being tied in below the knee. These are three common faults that want watching. Make sure, by standing in front, that the toes neither turn in nor out.

straight front legs

19

When thinking of buying a pony always ask someone to ride it for you first – *before* you ride it yourself. See it go through all its paces, and you will then get an idea of how it behaves, and it will also give you a chance to stand back and watch how it moves. You can then ride it yourself and see how it feels.

It is also worth while seeing the pony led up in hand. You can watch to see if it goes straight, and you can see if it is sensible about being led. Always see that this is done on a hard flat surface. You can then be really sure whether or not the pony is going *straight*.

Finally, before buying the pony it is well worth your while to ask your veterinary surgeon to examine it for you. It may save you a lot of money. And if you are buying it to show make quite sure that it will box easily. A lovely show pony is not a great deal of use just standing at home.

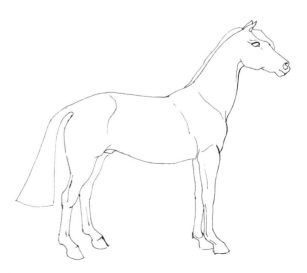

3 Schooling

Seldom is enough importance attached to the proper schooling of the pony, *on the ground*; by which we mean 'in hand', both in stable and out, as well as on the lunge.

Let us first of all take the handling of the pony 'in hand'. What one is really aiming at with a pony can be summed up in one word 'respect'. Once a pony has a real respect for its owner or rider then half the battle is won. But to gain this respect one must have endless patience, feeling (that is, sensitiveness) and authority.

    Authority in one's voice, like so many other things, is a gift or a knack. Either one has it or has not; but there can be no doubt that ponies, like children, are much happier if they know just where they are and exactly what is expected

In hand

21

from them. If one has authority in one's voice it is so much easier for a pony to know and to understand what he is being told. It is really quite easy to tell how a pony is treated and managed at home from the way he behaves when out and about.

In stable

When dealing with a pony in the stable be sure that he is kept up to the mark. In other words see that he 'moves over' when he is told to and *only* when he is told; see that he stands still when he is supposed to; see that he moves smartly, picks up his feet, turns or whatever it may be, when *you* want him to and not whenever *he* feels like it. This can only be achieved by patience and firmness – never by bullying or bad temper; but once achieved it will make stable-work far easier and much more enjoyable.

Tying-up

It will also prove a great help *outside* if he is used to and sensible about being tied up *inside*. Nothing is more annoying than a pony that is tiresome to tie up at a show or gymkhana. Running back on a halter is a particularly tiresome habit because so often, once a pony has done it and hurt himself, he is inclined to do it again and again. He has lost confidence. So with a halter, make sure first that the rope cannot tighten round his nose should he pull back. It is often wise to attach a thinner rope, such as baler-string, to the end of the halter rope, then if the pony does run back it breaks and he is not so frightened. If he is, he will not forget it and he will be just that much more of a handful.

slip knot; easy to tighten, by pulling the right end, and undo by pulling loose end

When teaching a pony what one might term 'stable manners', one must never be far away in case something unfortunate does happen; but it is wonderful how even the shyest and most nervous ponies soon settle down sensibly if they are regularly tied up in the yard with all the hustle-bustle of children and dogs, tractors, perhaps, and cars going on all around them.

Leading

It is vitally important that a pony in the show ring stands properly and leads well. So often one sees a pony being really awkward at this stage. It has gone well in the class; it has given quite a good individual show and then just when the time has come to clinch the matter before the judges, it behaves like a pig. It stands all lop-sided or drooping, or it doesn't stand at all. When its rider tries to lead it away from the judges it hangs back and refuses to follow. When it is run up at the trot, it gallivants sideways. All the earlier good impression is ruined.

A pony, therefore, should be taught to lead and to stand at home, and this most simple part of showing is more often forgotten than any other. Only by patience will you teach him to stand properly : equally on all four legs and without a lot of shuffling, shaking his head and nudging. No great skill is needed. It is simply a matter of making him understand that he is not to move unless he is told to. Tradesmen's ponies learn quickly enough : and look at the way a hunt servant's horse will stand when the huntsman or whipper-in has had to get off to deal with some matter. He will stand while all the rest of the field gallop past

London police horse

leading, the right way; the leader level with the pony's shoulder: right, leading, the wrong way

him or while an express train roars by. Look, too, at police horses and the mounted sentries in Whitehall. It is just a matter of patience and firmness again.

To teach him to lead well make him walk alongside you, not behind you. You should be level with his shoulder.

At first, while walking with him, carry a long stick; then if he starts to hang back as you move forward, just tickle him with the end of it behind his girth. He will very quickly realize what you mean and walk alongside you freely. Then when he is in the show ring with you, you can be confident that he will walk out, just as he does at home, and there will be none of this embarrassing tug-of-war. Remember, too, never to look back at him : always look forward in the direction you are going, and when you want to turn, turn him away from you. Don't pull him after you, because by doing this latter you are forcing him to lose his position which should be forward of you, your shoulder in line with his.

There can be no doubt whatever that any horse or pony that is going to appear in the show ring is going to benefit enormously from lunging. By lunging a horse one can teach him to move in a proper, balanced way; one can extend the length of his stride; and one can even improve his shape, because he is being made to use certain muscles, particularly the neck, shoulder and quarters, in a proper way. Unfortunately it is not easy to lunge well : and to lunge badly can do no good at all. But as a show pony can be so greatly improved by work on the lunge – and all the most successful ones have been – it is perhaps worth while giving a brief explanation of lunging and a few hints.

Lunging

To begin with, one can only really learn the art of lunging by doing it oneself. Then, if one is to be successful, one has to be able to see and to know just what one is looking for. Any pony can be taught to walk, trot and canter in an ordinary way just by use of the voice and simple aids. With a pony on the lunge one can see if the pony is really *working*. If he is, then he is all the time improving at every pace; and how a pony that really does use himself stands out in the show

25

ring, compared with the pony that just walks, trots and canters in the ordinary, humdrum way !

When first teaching a young pony to work on the lunge two people are essential. The first few lessons should be extremely simple, with one person in the centre holding the lunge rein and whip, and the other leading the pony on the outside by an ordinary rein attached to a snaffle bit. The pony is led quietly round in a circle, thus enabling him to be taught to walk on, and to halt.

This first stage can be taught surprisingly quickly, and very soon a pony can be allowed to go on its own. The lunge work, will, of course, be very much easier if you have taken the trouble to teach your pony to lead in hand, as then he already knows how to walk out and how and when to halt. He must never be allowed to trot or canter before he has properly learnt to walk on the lunge. If each stage is taken steadily, then your pony will not be one of those mad beasts who gallop wildly round as soon as you start off. So get the walk right first, and then the trot; and remember it will always take five or ten minutes for a pony really to settle down for his work. Never be in too much of a hurry : but at the same time do not be tempted to work your pony too long on the lunge each day; for it is very concentrated work and he could easily become bored which would, of course, produce just the wrong effect. About twenty minutes should be quite sufficient for the first few lessons.

To lunge a pony successfully you need a cavesson (see illustration), a long rein and a long, light stick with a leash on the end. A cavesson is, in our

one type of cavesson, strongly recommended because it is firm fitting and because the ring on the front gives the lunger excellent control
below; another type

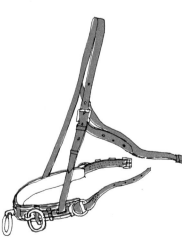

opinion, essential, although many people lunge off the lead collar – the cavesson, we believe is better, because (a) one has far more control, and (b) it fits snugly to the pony's head and so it cannot possibly slip over his eyes like a head collar. A long lunge rein which can easily be bought at any saddler's is absolutely essential; but do make sure that it is long enough : some are much shorter than others. A long stick is necessary too, so that one can touch the pony from the centre (the best kind looks like a ring master's whip, and they are exceptionally light). Some people prefer lunging on their own and in many ways it is better to have complete control – but some ponies can be very lazy, and then two people (one with the whip and one the lunge rein) are better. Single-handed one cannot drive the pony forward nearly as well. A point to remember is that if there are two of you it is just as important for the person holding the lunge rein to be as experienced as the person using his voice and holding the whip.

A few more vital things to remember : the pony must be kept out at the end of the rein; he must be made to work properly and not allowed to slop around; the person in the centre should stand absolutely still so that the pony forms a triangle with the whip and lunge rein. Remember never to get in front of him, otherwise it encourages him to stop and come in towards the centre.

It is so very easy to see a pony's faults on the lunge, e.g. where he is most stiff, either in his neck, or back, perhaps. Now this sort of fault

27

Top: lunging: first lesson — the pony is led round at the end of the lunge.

Below: the pony is now going freely, right out at the end of the lunge — in these pictures a particularly long lunge rein is being used; such a long rein is not easy if lunging single-handed

stops a pony being able to go at his best in the show ring. By lunging you can get your pony going *freely forward*, learning to have his own correct balance at all paces, the right bends on both reins and moving with freedom and smooth transitions at all paces. The lunge enables him to be free and encourages *free forward movement*. Without this one will never get very far in the show ring. Work on the lunge can help a tremendous amount to improve a pony. By gently sending a pony on, on the lunge, and thus encouraging him to stretch his neck forward, the shape of the neck, will, in time, alter, as the pony will have been made to use the right neck muscles. In the same way the back can be made to work as it should, and the whole body of the pony become nice and supple.

If lunged properly the faults of a pony can soon be overcome. Lunging is the shortest way round some of the commonest faults. You can get a pony working better in the correct way in shorter time on the lunge because it is easier to obtain his whole attention.

Patience, firmness and kindness are the most important factors if one wants good results. Always remember that every pony is different in temperament and so needs individual handling.

As we said earlier, lunging is difficult: it is also very controversial. For instance, experts are always ready to argue about the use of side-reins. In our own opinion, if a pony is to learn to mouth properly, then a snaffle bridle with reins running from the bit to fasten on a roller or saddle will act as a contact through the weight of the rein. This is an excellent way of teaching a pony to mouth, but it must be realized that the lunge rein must still come from the cavesson, never off the bit. A pony should never be lunged off the bit.

All this, of course, is somewhat technical, but today if you are going to get a pony to the top, nothing must be overlooked; and you will always be able to find someone experienced to help with your work on the lunge.

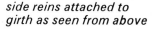

side reins attached to girth as seen from above

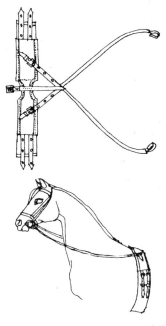

simple schooling in a snaffle at home – note the equine spectator nearby which helps to get a pony used to others while it is working and concentrating – so often a pony schooled on its own will nap when asked to leave others

SCHOOLING FROM ON TOP

Obviously, if one is going to school a pony for the show ring, especially if one is aiming at top-class shows, one must have a certain amount of knowledge. It is no good expecting a pony to canter with the proper leg leading, if you have no idea what the right aids are. First of all, therefore, you must make sure you know the right aids for all the movements you are likely to want him to perform. A competent rider can cover up so much if his or her pony is not going as well as it should. The rider's thoughts and wishes are very quickly conveyed to the pony, so that a calm, sensitive, quick-witted rider with a firm, decisive mind will teach a pony so much more quickly than the slow, impatient or fluffy type, who is incapable of communicating swiftly and accurately his wishes and commands to his pony.

If, therefore, you are going to school your own pony, it is essential that you should be quite clear yourself just what you want your pony to do. If you have been fortunate enough to have had your pony properly lunged or lunged it yourself, then your work on top will be very much easier.

The halt

First and very important, teach your pony to halt properly : to stand still squarely on all four legs, well on the bit, balanced and ready to move forward at the slightest pressure of the legs.

The walk

The walk should be free with even steps, the rider maintaining a light but steady contact on the mouth. Although a pony in the show ring should walk out, he does not want to be allowed to walk so fast as to lose his stride and appear to be waddling.

The trot

As with the walk, so the trot should be free, with even strides and, above all, balanced. When required to go into a stronger trot, the pony should extend his neck as he lengthens his stride. If a pony is not sufficiently trained to go into a stronger trot, you will find there is a tendency for him to go quicker and higher instead of longer. This should be resisted. It is a great mistake to force a pony into a strong trot before he is ready for it, as it will upset his balance and he will lose the even, easy rhythm that is essential, and so attractive to watch.

The canter

This pace should be absolutely free, a light contact being maintained on the mouth, so that one feels that one is being carried along. Above all, a pony should go *straight* at the canter. His rhythm should be smooth, with his own natural balance. If the pace is to be increased, it should be done calmly, smoothly, almost imperceptibly. Nothing looks worse than a pony gassing up the moment he is asked to go a little faster; but it is very common indeed, and judges note it and murmur to themselves 'Not really a *child's* pony,' and down the line it goes.

The rein-back

It is useless to attempt to rein-back until your pony has learnt first to halt correctly : balanced, well on the bit. When he can do this, then teach him to move back evenly, steadily in a straight line, his diagonal legs moving together. Always he must be steadily on the bit, so that at the first sign from his rider he will again move forward without hesitation. It is not at all easy to teach a pony to rein-back in a way which does not look ragged and untidy. It needs much practice.

The aids

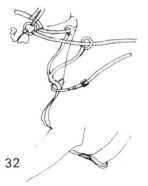

At this stage we must briefly mention the aids. These are the simple 'signals' that a rider must use if he wishes his mount to perform correctly the paces and movements that he requires. Obviously the simple aids have been outlined in many books, but this seems to us the proper place to mention them again, and to save our readers from searching through other books, we are here setting out briefly the principal aids in their two groups, the natural ones and the artificial.

32

(1) The natural aids are those through which the rider conveys his intentions to the horse and which the pony must learn to obey and understand. They employ the hands, the legs, the body and the voice.

(2) The artificial aids are such things as whips, spurs, martingale, gags. The use of the whip and voice are very helpful for preliminary training with a young horse, so that through them he can learn to understand the natural aids. Artificial aids must be used with great care, as misuse of them can lead to extreme unkindness to a pony.

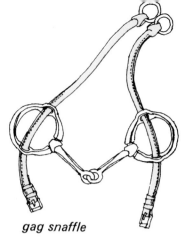

gag snaffle

Natural aids

The legs help to guide and control the quarters; they also create impulsion.

The hands, in conjunction with legs, regulate the effort created by the legs; they also help to control the forehand and can guide and control the pace.

The body by distribution of its weight forward, backward or sidewards, helps the animal to carry out what is being asked of him. The weight of the body should be going very slightly in the direction of the movement.

The voice, particularly in teaching a young pony, if used the right way, is a great help. A firm voice is extremely important when handling a pony on the ground, and it can assist in giving confidence to a nervous type of pony.

The correct aids for the different paces are as follows:

Walk. Shorten up your reins to the proper length, squeeze with both legs and drive forward with seat and legs. When the pony moves forward relax pressure with legs, but maintain contact with the reins so as to proceed at the pace required.

Trot. If going from a walk, remember first to shorten up the reins, then use the same aids as for the walk. To go into a strong trot – very effective in the show ring – use more pressure with legs. The pony will want to use a little more length of rein as he stretches forward his neck, but it is very important to maintain the same feel on the reins.

Canter. If using the *diagonal* aids, the simplest way to remember the aids is : first the rider should cease trotting and sit down in the saddle; then use the outside leg behind the girth and the inside one very slightly on the girth. The weight of the body also shifts slightly on the outside seat bone. Never look down to see on to which leg the pony has led.

Halt. Use both legs; resist with hands; bring weight of body very slightly back. This drives the pony up to his bit, which means that he will halt with a steady head, his weight on *all* legs.

Rein-Back. He must step back with an even rhythm, so be sure that he is steady at the halt first; then bring slight pressure with your legs until you feel him about to move; now relax the leg pressure but maintain feel on reins. It should be maintained for as many steps back as you wish your pony to move. By the pressure of your legs in a firm position – not forward or right back – he will be kept straight.

4 Turn-out of pony and rider

a well-turned-out combination that could not fail to catch a judge's eye

However well a pony may be schooled, it is still going to be of the utmost importance that he is properly presented in the show ring. It is important, therefore, that both pony and rider should be properly turned out. Judges are very human. Inevitably they are influenced by the

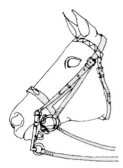

a double bridle

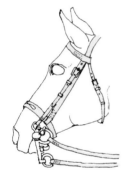

a pelham bit

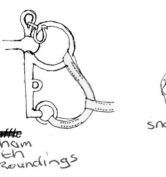

a ~~snaffle~~
Pelham
with
Roundings

appearance of those parading before them. If riders and ponies are correctly dressed and turned out, the judges feel that they must be exhibitors of experience, and are accordingly influenced.

A pony should always be shown in a bridle with two reins, either an ordinary double or a 'pelham'. The double bridle, of course, is best, but sometimes a pony goes better in a pelham, though a judge seeing a pony in a pelham may wonder if it is really a child's pony. In 12·2 classes, when the riders are only twelve or younger, a single rein is permitted. In leading rein classes, which become more and more popular every year, a new rule has been introduced by the British Show Pony Association saying that all ponies must wear plain snaffle bridles.

Saddlery is very expensive these days, of course, but if properly looked after can always look nice, even though it may not be the best of its kind.

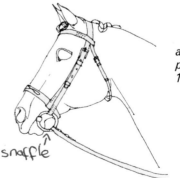

snaffle

a single rein is permitted in 12·2 classes

36

The ideal show bridle is stitched and does not have buckles or studs as it then looks neater. The leather should not be too thick, as the thinner and lighter it is the prettier it looks. The nose-band can either be separate or, if preferred, stitched running through the cheek piece and thus saving an extra strap over the head piece. The buckles and bit are best in stainless steel, as it is easier to clean. Plated bits can be used, of course, but though they have a wonderful glinting finish, the plate tends to peel off them in quite a short time, and they are not really to be recommended.

A coloured brow-band is always effective and really does not cost very much in the way of trouble. Some people use a plastic brow-band, but it is nicer to have a home-made ribbon one, using perhaps the stable colours or a colour scheme that matches the pony.

A martingale is not allowed in the show ring except in such classes as juvenile working-hunter classes, when the exhibitors are asked to jump.

Be sure that the bridle fits correctly. There should be room for four fingers, or the breadth of the hand, beneath the throat lash (always allow sufficient room for the pony to bend his neck). With the nose-band, there should be two fingers' width from the front, for the tightness; and two fingers from the bottom of the side-cheek bone, for the height. This must particularly be remembered if one is having a stitched nose-band made to run through the cheek piece.

The bit wants to lie so that it does not wrinkle the corners of the mouth, but not so low that it allows the tongue to get over it. The curb chain

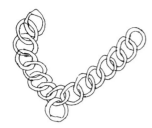

curb chain

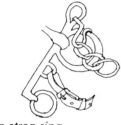

lip strap ring

must lie flat with the centre ring hanging down and with the lip strap running through it. Nothing looks more untidy or, indeed, careless than a twisted curb chain. Equally bad is the absence of the lip strap. If the curb is not correctly fitted, it can be painful for a pony and it will soon make him sore. It will hardly be surprising then if he becomes difficult. To put the curb chain on correctly, first get the chain straight from end to end; then fasten one end on to the hook and then fix the other end on. Choose whichever ring is the right one for the length you want and loop it on. Make sure that the lip strap ring is hanging on the lower side.

The saddle

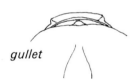

gullet

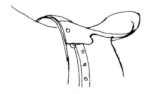

straight cut flap

The most important thing is to see that the saddle is not so low down on the withers that it can make the pony sore. Obviously if a pony is to give of his best he must be comfortable. Be sure, too, that it is possible to see daylight right through the gullet; otherwise a pony will be pinched and will soon get a sore back.

If a saddle sits too far up the withers with forward flaps, then there is a likelihood that it will detract from, rather than flatter, a pony's front. Try to buy or borrow a saddle that sits well down behind the pony's shoulder. This probably means a straight cut flap.

The rider should, of course, sit right in the middle of the saddle, but often a saddle is so made that it is quite impossible for a rider to sit in the centre of it. So often it just is not appreciated how much this can mar one's chances in the show ring.

There are three possible linings for a saddle: leather, linen and serge. Leather, of course, is the easiest to clean, but linen or serge are softer on a pony's back. A good saddle, if carefully looked after, can last for years and can therefore be regarded as a good investment. If you are going to buy one, always take with you some-one knowledgeable who can tell the saddler exactly what is wanted. There is always a good sale for secondhand saddles as long as they are in good condition, which means that when you have grown out of one, or have got a new pony which needs a saddle of a different shape, there is no reason why you should not get your money back.

. . sit in the centre of it . . .

Stirrups

The best kind of stirrups are steel ones, although they are a little more expensive. A nickel stirrup *can* buckle should you be unfortunate enough to have a fall, and then, of course, your foot could be caught in it.

Girths

It is a matter of choice which kind of girth you have; but once again the thinner and lighter type of girth will always make a pony look smarter. Today nylon girths are very popular, as they wash easily, are not too expensive, and on ponies that are rather fat and soft they are less likely to give girth galls. A thin white webbing girth looks very smart on a show pony and is becoming increasingly popular.

One last point about a pony's equipment: very small ponies sometimes use a crupper, but these should not be used in the show ring.

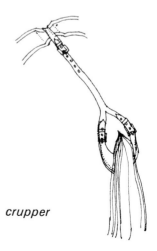

crupper

THE RIDER

The rider can make or mar a pony's chances so much more than is usually realized. A young rider smartly and efficiently turned out cannot help but catch the judge's eye, so it is well worth taking a little trouble.

Riding clothes can be expensive, but even old clothes can look perfectly presentable if well cleaned and properly worn.

It goes without saying that in an ordinary show class just as much as in a gymkhana or show jumping, a hard hat is absolutely essential. A velvet hunting cap is the most usual and certainly the most comfortable. If a bowler hat is worn it must be worn correctly, not at an angle, not on the back of the head and not with an elastic under the chin; it should also be a good shape. An elastic under the chin should never be worn in the show ring.

If the rider is a girl, she must be sure that her hair is tidy. A small girl need not wear a hair-net, but older girls should if their hair is anything but very short. Short, curly hair showing under a velvet cap can look very smart. Longer hair should be tied back.

bowler

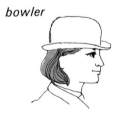

Coat   A white shirt with a dark tie will always look smarter than a coloured shirt. Either a tweed or a navy blue coat can be worn. For smaller shows, the former is adequate, but at the big shows navy-blue is definitely more correct. In our opinion a black coat is never quite right for a child.

40

All the buttons on the coat should be done up (in a turn-out class marks can be taken off for the buttons left undone).

The tie-pin is better worn crossways, as in an accident an up-and-down tie-pin can cut into the chin, or into the stomach.

Gloves

A nice pair of gloves always looks smart. They can be of string, and white, brown, yellow or grey in colour: white or yellow are smartest. Leather or pig-skin gloves are also popular, and the latter especially look very professional and are comfortable to wear with reins. So often gloves are left off, but they are really an essential part of show wear.

Stick

A proper riding stick should always be carried – not a switch or a cutting whip nor, in the show ring, a hunting crop. A little leather stick is always correct, or a blackthorn one. The correct way to hold one is in the middle, so that approximately the same amount of stick shows either side of the hand. If it sticks out too high it looks like a fishing-rod: if too low, like a racing whip. A discerning judge will notice which hand it is carried in. There are times when a pony's behaviour will necessitate its being changed.

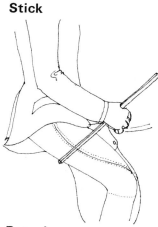

Breeches

Most children, of course, wear jodhpurs and very smart they can look. Very *un*smart too. They must be nicely fitting, rather on the tight side, in fact, as nothing looks worse than sloppy jodhpurs, baggy in the legs, baggy in the bulge and baggy in the seat. For showing,

41

the summer weight material is the most practical.

If breeches are worn they, too, want to be well-fitting, and it is most important to see that they are buttoned in the proper position, i.e. the *inside* of the knee, not the outside. Breeches and boots should only be worn by older children and it is, in our opinion, preferable for all children in pony classes to wear jodhpurs. After all, the oldest children in the 14·2 hands classes are only fifteen years old. They will have plenty of time for breeches and boots as adults.

Boots

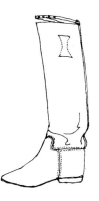

It is best that proper jodhpur boots or lace-up boots are worn with jodhpurs, not shoes. An expanse of ankle and sock between the shoe and the jodhpur turn-up looks so bad in the show ring. If boots are worn they must be the right size – father's will look like gum-boots on a child! – and really well cleaned, as they are very much in evidence. Garters must be worn, and should have the buckle between the top two buttons of the breeches, with the strap going towards the outside. Spurs, of course, should only be worn with top-boots, not with jodhpur boots.

To complete the ensemble a small button-hole, a rose bud or a cornflower, or something small that matches the pony's brow-band, is effective: but not a great bouquet.

Proper turn-out means a lot of trouble, but it is worth it and your pony deserves it.

5 Preparation before a show

Obviously if you hope to do well with your
pony at a show he must look at his very best.
So often one sees a nice pony lose all chance of
winning just because he is looking rather scraggy
and is badly turned out. It is surprising how a
less high-class pony will often be a place or two
higher in a show simply because the owner has
taken the trouble to have him looking really
well and behaving properly.

It is often the trimming that gives the
complete finishing touch – that just makes the
difference, in fact, between a first and a second
rosette.

The heels, of course, will always have to be
trimmed for a show : untidy heels suggest lack
of quality. Either use clippers or scissors and
a comb. But be careful if using clippers not to
leave a hard line where the clippers finish
cutting.

Trimming

43

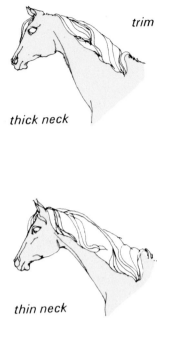

trim

thick neck

thin neck

Next, trimming on the withers and behind the poll, where the headpiece of the bridle goes. It is surprising how much you can do by trimming carefully in these places to improve and help the shape of a pony's neck. If a pony is a little stuffy and fat in the neck, then you must take especial care to make the neck look as swan-like as possible; in which case you may have to cut as much as three or four inches on the withers in order to help the shoulder line, where the neck meets the shoulder. By trimming a little more than usual at the top of the neck, you will make the neck look slim. To heighten this effect trim as close to the skin as possible.

If a pony has rather a thin or mean neck, then do *not* shave him clean at the withers and behind the poll. Leave only half an inch or so at the withers to make him appear to have more substance than in fact he has.

If a pony's neck is not his strong point, then plaiting is most essential. The thicker, short-necked pony must have small, tight, neat plaits, that lie as close as possible to the neck line. The thin-necked pony can have more chunky plaits, which give the effect of looking bigger in the neck.

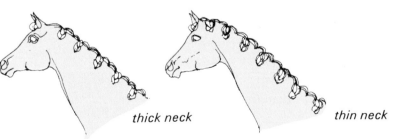

thick neck   *thin neck*

Before plaiting up, the mane must have been properly pulled. Pulling a mane is not at all difficult once you have been shown how. The manes of some of the native breed ponies are often so thick that it is really impossible to plait them unless they have been well pulled first.

Never use scissors on a mane. All that is required is a mane-comb. By thinning out the long pieces and gently pulling them out from the *roots*, you can level the mane to the length required. Unless you pull them out from the roots you will get a bitty and uneven mane. Ponies do not, as a rule, mind having their manes pulled and it can easily be done in one go. If a pony should be difficult, however, it is better to do it in several goes, so that the pony does not get irritated and fed up with it, because if he does, next time will be harder.

A really well-pulled tail is tremendously important, because it can improve the appearance of a pony's hind quarters: indeed it can give a pony more quality altogether.

Pulling a tail is not really difficult, but people often fight shy of starting on a really thick tail, as they are so afraid that they might pull the wrong pieces out. In fact, at the beginning, it is impossible to go wrong, as so much has got to come out. It is nearer the end that it becomes more difficult.

Decide first what shape you want, so that you don't pull too far down. It takes some time for the long pieces to grow again if you have pulled them out by mistake. It is not easy to

Manes and tails

mane comb

pulling a mane

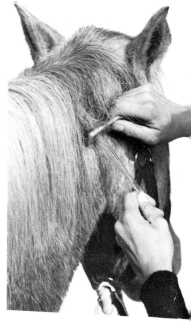

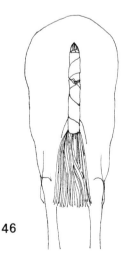

washing the tail – note that the tail is well in the bucket

explain exactly how to pull a tail – it is best to get someone with experience to show you; but the few points that follow will help you.

Do not pull out too much in one go. It will possibly need four or five goes if the tail is really thick.

After the first attempt, wash the tail and bandage it. This will give you a better idea of the shape you are getting at.

Be sure not to pull so much out that you get bare patches. A well-pulled tail has just a covering of hair along the pulled part of the dock, and viewed from the side should have no short pieces hanging down (girls with 'swept-up' hair-styles under velvet caps please note!).

The art of a well-pulled tail is have no skirt line: which means that the short pieces should mould smoothly into the longer ends of the tail.

This can be encouraged by always bandaging right to the bottom of the dock.

The average length for a tail is down to the chestnuts (just below the hocks): but one has to take into account how each particular pony carries his tail. Some ponies carry their tails much higher than others.

Finally, when cutting the bottom of the tail, remember to cut slightly on the slant, because the tail, when it is carried, is at a slightly different angle from when lying flat in the dock.

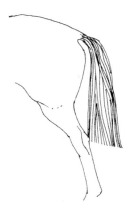

Head

Ears always want trimming, especially if they are on the large size; it can improve the appearance of the head surprisingly. Too much should not be trimmed out of the centre, particularly if a pony is living out. It has been given hair in its ears for a purpose – namely, protection.

All that remains now to be trimmed is under the jaw and round the muzzle.

The better bred pony has very little hair to tidy up under the jaw, but if the jaw is being trimmed, remember not to make ugly scissor marks. All the whiskers should come off round the muzzle, but it is not kind, surely, to remove them from round the eyes. They are there not only for protection, but also in some way for feeling.

Cleaning

If a pony is living out, then it is obviously unwise to remove all the natural grease from its coat by cleaning it the day before the show, as if it is not too warm at night it may well catch cold.

47

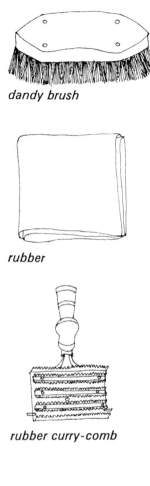

dandy brush

rubber

rubber curry-comb

water brush

Wisping and banging

Assuming, however, that the pony is lying in, here is how to clean up the pony before the show.

Get all the exercising done in the morning if possible – before breakfast, if school time has to be coped with – then the rest of your time can be devoted to the pony and the tack.

If the day is warm it is far easier to clean the pony when it is tied up in the stable yard. First, either with the dandy brush or rubber curry-comb, remove all the surplus mud, sweat and loose hairs (the rubber curry-comb is excellent for removing loose hairs and sweat, and ponies generally prefer it to the dandy brush). Then, using the water brush, remove all stains or straighten out any ruffled hair. A square of sacking that is just damp is an excellent sub-stitute for the water brush, although it is not a recognized part of grooming equipment. It is also excellent for cleaning a very greasy pony; for example, a pony that is out at grass and wants cleaning in one day for a show, will obviously be very greasy if it has not recently had much grooming. The sack used, just damp, in a circular movement going both ways on the hair seems to remove a lot of the grease under the coat, which is such hard work to remove by body brush.

Next wisp your pony, either with a plain hay wisp or one wrapped in a damp sack. This helps to do two jobs in one: as the pony is benefiting from the wisping, you might say it is being both polished and massaged. Wisping or 'banging'

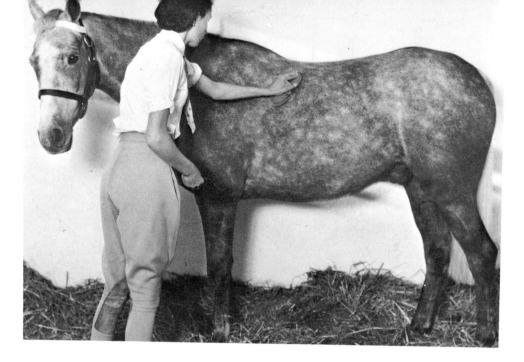

using the body brush – plenty of elbow grease needed – notice how the groom is using the correct hand on the correct side

is most important, for as well as massaging the skin it helps to develop and harden the muscles; and in banging the skin it squeezes the oil out and so improves the shine on the coat. There is, of course, a real art in wisping the correct way. The whole arm should be used in wisping or banging, so that it is more of a movement employing the weight of the whole body rather than just hitting. If done correctly it should not be at all tiring. If it is too exhausting, in fact, then you may be sure that you are not doing it right.

The bangs should be even and not too quick, but hard enough to make the muscles work by reacting to the impact of the bang. It is quite

The body brush should be cleaned frequently with the curry comb

Patient banging possible to test for oneself how effective one's banging is being: by stopping just as you are about to bang the pony, one should be able to see the muscles react in anticipation. By concentrating on the weaker parts of the pony – the muscles at the top of the neck, for example, because they are the neck muscles that a pony should be using, or the muscles on the hind quarters – it is quite remarkable how these muscles can be rounded and strengthened by patient banging. Done for twenty or thirty minutes at a time, twice a day, and with the addition, of course, of careful feeding, a big improvement will be achieved in a short time.

One must *never* bang on the loins, as this could hurt a horse, and obviously the bony parts of a horse will not need banging.

When the banging is finished, then use the body brush, with the curry-comb to clean it. Some people wisp and bang *after* using the body brush, but we are of the opinion that if using a damp sack or wisp it tends to leave patches or bits of hay which can be cleaned away by using the body brush after the wisp.

Body brushing *is* hard work, but a real lot of elbow grease *is* necessary if you want to get a pony clean.

Finish off with a rubber. It is not enough just to wipe your pony over: use more of the wisping movement again and it will help to bring up the bloom on his coat.

Some people, again, prefer to wash first, but if a
pony is already really clean then there is no
possibility of dust from grooming settling back
when the pony has been washed.

The mane should be washed about once a
fortnight and preferably *not* the day before a
show, as it makes plaiting up more difficult –
just as it is difficult to make one's hair behave
properly just after a shampoo!

Detergents for washing manes are not
recommended, as they are so hard on the skin.
But excellent animal shampoos are available in
various sized tins, and in the end it is more
economical to use one, and better for the pony

You will need two buckets of warm water,
a sponge, soap, a towel and a sweat scraper.

Using the water and a large sponge, wet the
mane, thoroughly wash and then rinse with
fresh water. Don't be afraid really to soak the
mane. It may soak the neck and face as well,
but most ponies do not mind. A towel can be used
to dry the mane, and a sweat scraper to remove
surplus water from the neck.

The tail should be washed in exactly the same
way : but remember to put the tail right into the
bucket so that the dock gets really clean: and
it is most important to rinse thoroughly. One
often sees lumps of scurf in a tail which are due
to soap being left in.

Get all the surplus water out of the tail by
whirling the end of the tail with your hands.

If the legs are very dirty they, too, should
be washed: it can do no harm, unless one forgets
really to dry out the heels afterwards. If this is

forgotten cracked heels may result; and nothing is more painful for a pony.

Grey ponies need particular attention because of the stains, but always remember that if the weather is cold and a pony is not properly dried, just like human beings he can catch cold. So walk the pony round well to dry him off, and keep him warm.

The pony, having been trimmed, groomed and washed, should now be looking extremely smart. To test your thoroughness, take a clean white rubber, give him a final polish and then see if the clean white rubber is still really clean!

If your pony is living in at night before a show, put four stable bandages on him to keep his legs clean. Gamgee tissue under the bandages is a good idea, if you consider it worth the slight additional expense.

Give him a generous bed of really clean straw, and then the final cleaning in the morning will not be such hard work. A summer sheet too will help to keep him clean: but whatever you do and however hard you have worked, there will still be that final effort in the morning.

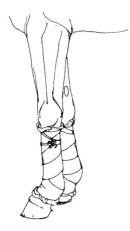

Tack cleaning

This very elementary subject has been dealt with thoroughly in so many books that it merits only a passing reference in this book, which is dealing specifically with showing.

To most children and young people the cleaning of tack is very boring and something to be avoided if it can possibly be organized, only really getting down to it before some big function. As a result the standard of tack-cleaning that one sees in the show ring is not very high, as unless tack is cleaned regularly it will never look very good, however hard one works at the last minute.

To clean a saddle or bridle really well is something of an art. If one takes the trouble to learn the correct method and then practises it, it is not difficult or very hard work – no more hard work in fact than the effort taken to clean a saddle and bridle badly so that it looks as if it has hardly been cleaned at all, still appearing all dry and hard and musty.

If your saddle and bridle are really properly looked after it will save you a lot of money in the long run, because it is lack of regular attention that makes harness crack and break,

the harness-room: hard at work – nothing is too unimportant to be neglected when it comes to preparing for the show ring

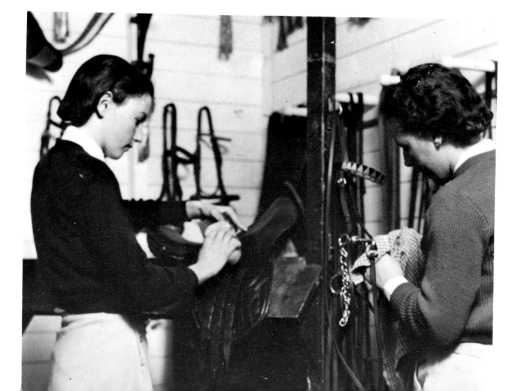

whereas regular attention keeps it supple and soft as well as clean.

For showing tack, which should, of course, be kept particularly well, here are a few points worth remembering.

Oils for leather Unfortunately a new saddle or a new bridle never looks very nice on a pony, as the colour is rather ugly and it is inclined to be stiff and to squeak. Various oils can be used to tone down the colour and soften the leather : linseed oil, neat's-foot oil and Ko-cho-line. In our opinion nothing is better than the first, as it brings the leather to a lovely colour, whereas neat's-foot oil makes it very dark. Ko-cho-line seems to leave it a little sticky. One or two good goes with linseed oil and the leather turns a beautiful light brown colour, at the same time becoming really soft.

Most people would agree that new tack is not only ugly to look at, but it is really not very nice to ride with.

The bridle should frequently be taken to pieces and cleaned, otherwise the buckles become very hard and sometimes rusty. This looks very bad.

In cleaning, the most important thing is soaping. Use a soap sponge, really well wrung out, as leaving lather on a bridle not only makes it sticky instead of soft and pliable, but the lather also gets stuck in the holes.

The buckles and bits should be metal-polished and really shine; but never metal-polish the piece that actually goes into the mouth: ponies do not always like the taste of metal-polish.

Never leave tack lying on the ground – and that includes the saddle. Even if it is stood up the right way against a stone wall it can get scratched. Either place it on a rug or hang it up.

Other show accessories such as head collar, knee pads, rollers should also be properly cleaned. A head collar always looks well if it has been soaped on the inside and polished on the outside with ordinary boot-polish. If there is anything that needs whitening, it should be done with a white boot-cleaning liquid, or a white powder slab.

In cold weather tack should always be kept somewhere where it is warm and properly heated. Even in a day or two it can go mouldy if left in the damp and it really can get into a sorry state. When tack is not being used, see that the position of the buckles is altered so that the leather round the usual hole is not being permanently marked – and worn. Obviously when used on your pony the straps will be in the same holes. But when the bridle is put on another pony requiring different lengths on the various straps, then the old holes will look very marked. So alter the buckles from time to time.

6 The morning of the show

It is only very hard-bitten types that do not wake up to a certain feeling of excitement and anticipation on the morning of a show. It is always a thrill, and it should be, for once a person becomes blasé about it and over-confident he does seem to lose that little bit of tension which all artists must possess, and which the *rider* will communicate to his horse or pony. It is in just the same way that the great actor always feels slightly nervous before going on the stage, and he will not be at his best unless he does.

The trouble is, of course, that if you are feeling excited about a show it is very difficult to sleep well, so that you may be exhausted when the time of your class actually comes. But try to go to bed early, so that you can easily get up early, as you will certainly have to. Often if you find you can't get to sleep and keep on waking up, then it is just at the time that you really want to wake up that you fall into the deepest sleep. So be sure to have an alarm-clock and test it properly: even the best alarm-clocks have a habit of ringing at unexpected times. If we have to be up really early we generally take the precaution of arranging with the telephone operator to call us as well. There is a small charge for this service and it can be relied on to be punctual.

Get as much as you can ready the night before, so that you do not take up precious minutes look-ing for socks and belts and boot-garters. Have everything laid out in its proper place and so save yourself valuable minutes, for however long you allow yourself, you will find that you are pushed for time.

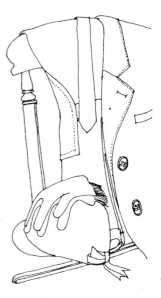

The stables

Depending chiefly on how long you take to plait a pony's mane, the time you must allow from the moment you get up till the moment you depart will be something rather more than an hour and a half. You may have to catch your pony in the field, bring him in and groom him; and if the weather is wet and he is very muddy, this will take a long time. It is essential to groom him *before* plaiting him up, otherwise all the dust and dirt when you are grooming him will go into the plaits and be difficult to get out.

It is perhaps more likely that you will have kept your pony in overnight, after all the hard work expended on him the evening before.

The first thing to do, then, on arriving at the stables is to remove all the droppings and wet straw as quickly as possible. With such a long day ahead, you may not want to use up all your energies on mucking out, but it is better to get it done. It may be that a pony lies down again, perhaps in a wet patch, even after you have finished, so make sure you remove any last-minute stains.

Plaiting

The following will be your essential requirements for plaiting: darning-size needle; thread to match the mane; scissors; mane comb; bucket of water.

If you are rather small, or your pony is rather big, it is always easier to stand on something to plait, so that you are plaiting from above; therefore have handy a chair or a stool or a strong box.

Unless you are very experienced, it is advisable to plan out your plaits, so that you can be sure of having the right number, rightly spaced out. This can be done with strong rubber bands. It will only take you a moment or two and can be a great help.

Using a single or a double thread according to its strength, with a knot at the end of it, start with the *forelock*. Wet it well with water first, then start plaiting.

Having done the forelock, starting from the poll, complete the other plaits down the neck.

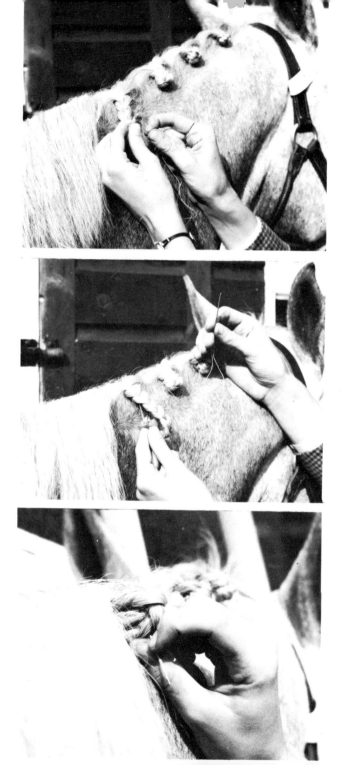

wind the thread
several times round
the bottom of the
plait and turn the
short, loose ends up

wind thread round
again to leave no
loose ends
turn plait under and
stitch round two or
three times
turn plait under
again and stitch
securely in place

how far under you
turn each time
depends on the length
of the mane and the
size of the
plait required

59

Have the thread as near as possible the same colour as the mane. Plait as tightly as possible. Have as little thread showing as you possibly can. When *un*plaiting after the show, be careful not to cut off any of the mane, or after a very few times of plaiting you will find yourself left with a very bitty mane. Never leave the plaits in longer than is necessary, as they will get rubbed and the mane will break at the top. *Never* cut the odd bits sticking up along the top of the mane. This is really fatal for future efforts. Either encourage them into the plait, or if necessary *pull* them right out. Loose plaits with a looping effect are very unflattering to a pony's neck. Learn how to make them as neat as you can.

Grooming

If your pony has been standing in at night, then because of all the work you put in on the previous evening, he will not in the morning need a great deal of grooming.

Go quickly over him with the dandy brush; then either with the water brush or sack, straighten out any ruffled hair sticking up where he has been lying down.

Next use the body brush, and rub over; if your work was thorough the previous evening it can only be surface dust that has collected. Basically he should still be clean.

When you have finished with the pony, before thinking about yourself, it is advisable to check that absolutely everything is completely ready in the stable. You then know exactly how much time you have got left.

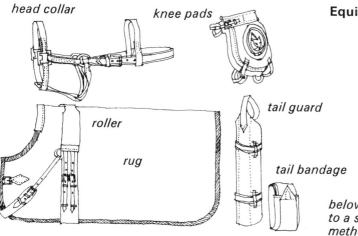

head collar *knee pads* **Equipment for pony**

roller

rug

tail guard

tail bandage

below, ready for boxing to a show – notice the method of bandaging, the knee pads, and the tail guard

Often people just put a pony in a box with nothing but a halter. This is a risk, because if he does get down he may well hurt himself. (Travelling a young unbroken pony is different. It is safer if he is completely loose in a big box with not even a partition. He is much less likely to be frightened by wearing things he is unused to or being strangely confined.)

Having put all the equipment on the pony, give him his breakfast and leave him in peace.

But in case he gets down and rolls, it is perhaps wisest to tie him up before you leave him.

Grooming equipment

You have still to collect and have ready your tack and grooming equipment, which you will want to take with you. If there is no place to hang up your tack in the horse-box, then it is best to wrap it all up in a rug, making sure that nothing gets dirty or scratched. Try to find a good-sized box with a handle and a lid that is big enough to keep all the grooming kit in. It makes it far less likely for things to get lost.

Take all your grooming kit together with some oil for the feet, Vaseline for the face and your plaiting equipment, just in case a plait comes undone. You may want to undo the plaits at the end of the show before a long journey home.

Be sure to take a full haynet, and a feed in a bucket; or if your pony is not going to need a feed, still take a bucket as it will be useful for water.

Completely satisfied that all is now ready, you can relax for a few moments, while you go in and have your own breakfast and get yourself ready.

The rider

However excited or however much in a hurry you may be, try and eat a proper breakfast. Every girl or boy going to a show is told that a hundred times. But it is sound advice, because it is likely that you will have so much to do once you are at the show, that you will have no time for a proper lunch. If you have not had a proper breakfast and have got up at about six o'clock, by the time it comes to your class you will be feeling quite weak, and that may prevent you from doing yourself proper justice.

The personal equipment that you are most likely to forget or mislay at the last moment includes your cap, your hair-net, your gloves, your showing stick. Know where they are so that there is no chance of your going without them. Be sure that your tie is properly pinned down. A flapping tie looks so untidy. If you have

Riding to the show

decided to wear a button-hole, select it and pre-pare it the night before. If you rush out into the garden just as you are going and seize a rosebud, you will probably find that by the time you get to the show it has turned out to be a full-blown rose. It does not look very good to have a great bouquet in your buttonhole. A single tight rose-bud with a single leaf, or two or three corn-flowers, or a small carnation is quite sufficient.

If the show is near enough for you to ride your pony there, rather than go in a box or trailer, it is most important that you leave more than enough time: otherwise your pony will arrive in a sweat and that will give you a lot of extra work before you go into the ring. Indeed, there may not even be time to cool him down and clean him.

If you can possibly arrange it, ride your pony in a different bridle from the one in which you are going to show him, and you will then have a nice clean bridle for the show itself.

7 In the ring

unboxing a pony

A few moments before your class actually enters the ring you will be called to the collecting ring. Be ready. Do not leave everything to the last minute, for there is nothing worse than arriving breathless just as your class is going in, having had no time to check over everything and get yourself and your pony into a calm and steady frame of mind.

Each rider knows his own pony's temperament best and will have learnt from experience how much work he wants before going into the ring.

This work is very important : it settles a pony, it gets him going properly, it tells the rider what sort of mood the pony is in – rather fresh, a little lazy, and so on.

It probably works out better if you work your pony first and then knock off, leaving yourself plenty of time to give him his final groom and clean up and to get yourself ready.

When doing your work – anything up to half an hour – try and keep out of people's way. Collisions can end in kicking matches, angry exchanges and an upset to pony and rider; and of course all the working-in wants to be in slow paces.

Preparations

Having rubbed the pony down after his work, oil his feet and Vaseline round the eyes and nostrils. A little Vaseline rubbed gently on can give a touch of glamour to a pony's face.

You may think it a good idea to make patterns on your pony's quarters. Not only does it look smart, but it also can improve the shape of a pony's quarters. It is not easy to put these patterns on, nor do they show up particularly well on a cold day when the coat is staring or stands up, or on a pony with a thick coat, or which has a winter coat coming through. It is a waste of time putting them on a dirty pony : it simply shows up the dirt!

You can either put on squares, which can be of any size you require and are put on the top of the quarters; or shark's teeth, which are put on down the flanks. Squares are the more simple to put on. All that is needed is an ordinary comb,

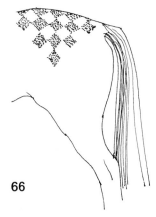

broken down to the correct size (obviously for ponies the squares will not want to be too big). As it is easier to put them on from above, you will be well advised to stand on a bucket to make your squares, or even bring a stool with you in the box.

First draw a line with your comb straight down the quarters, so that each side starts the same distance from the spine. The final result should look like a chess-board, working gradually down to one square at the bottom.

Shark's teeth, or triangles, are put on with a body brush.

Sponge out the pony's nostrils and mouth, seeing that the bit is clean; make sure his feet are picked out and no wisps of hay or straw are left in his tail.

Now you can turn to yourself. See that your hair is tidy, your shoes clean, your button-hole is in place. Tie on your number neatly. How often competitors forget their number until the last minute, or even altogether. The collecting-ring steward has every right to refuse admission to anyone without a number.

Go into the collecting ring in good time. Walking round with the other ponies and so close to the main ring acts as a dress-rehearsal, as one is all but experiencing the atmosphere of the show ring itself. Be friendly and natural with your opponents. It looks so bad to see children critically eyeing other ponies; or worse, two or three openly criticizing another. And whatever you do never show your superiority to someone less

Collecting-ring

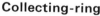

67

*elegant turn out
at Windsor Show*

fortunate than yourself on their rougher pony. It may be as good a *child's* pony as the more high-class one. In any case they are just as anxious to do well as you are.

The entrance

You will have made up your mind whether or not you want to go in first, when you get the word. Some ponies go better in front, hot up less. If yours is like that, keep him near the entrance as the class before you finishes. Some

line-up of ponies at the
South of England Show

ponies are lazy in front and brighten up with a
lead; in which case make sure that you are not
too near the entrance, or the steward may insist
on your pony going in first.

Wherever you go in see that you have plenty
of room between you and the pony in front of
you. The judges want to be able to have a good
look at you, and they cannot if you are all
bunched. Moreover, your pony will go better if
he is not right on another pony's heels.

69

The walk Make your pony walk in boldly and steadily and do not let him jib. First impressions are terribly important, and so much of the judge's opinion will be formed by what he sees of you at the walk. If you walk quicker than the pony in front, be absolutely sure that you do not get behind him, so that the judge cannot see. Better to pull back just before you come right in front of the judges, so that they look at you when your pony is walking nicely. If you can work it, see that you are not immediately behind one of the better ponies, because then you may not compare so well when the judges turn their eyes to you. If

a 12·2 hands pony demonstrating the correct paces for the show ring: walk . . .

it *can* be managed, get behind a less good pony!

Probably the judges will ask you to walk round in a small circle rather than right round the ring. Be on alert all the time, or you will look rather silly if you are the only one going round the outskirts of the ring. And try to look re-laxed and happy. It will suggest to the judge that you are confident and that your pony is giving you enjoyment, as a *child's* pony should.

a 14·2 hands pony demonstrating the correct paces for the show ring: walk . . .

The trot 'Trot on!' and immediately you will go into a larger circle. Obviously different ponies trot at different speeds, but at the trot it is more than ever important not to bunch. Many judges decide at the trot which ponies can really move, so if they are all bunched up they will never be able to see them properly, and a good pony can be missed altogether.

To avoid bunching you may be able to be crafty and cut a corner to get into a clear space, or go right round the outside to lose a group of two or three who are getting in your way. If you are out of sight of the judges, it is even permis-

a 12·2 hands pony demonstrating the correct paces for the show ring: trot . . .

sible to go round in a small circle on your own at the end of the ring. But at all costs, avoid bunching.

Some ponies look their best trotting on, others trotting more slowly. You will know which suits your pony best and try to keep him at his best pace. There is always a tendency to trot too fast, and often poor ponies hardly know what to do with their quarters at such speed: they are quite unbalanced.

a 14·2 hands pony demonstrating the correct paces for the show ring: trot . . .

The canter

Do not try to canter too slowly, as it makes a pony fussy, or even hot up, especially if others pass you. It will also shorten his stride. The canter wants, above all, to be fluent and look comfortable. A very short-stride canter never does.

The judges may ask you to change the rein. Be particularly careful not to make a muddle of your change of leg in sight of the judges. If you are absolutely sure that you can do a really smooth change, then, of course, it will look very impressive if you do your change right in front of the judges. The judges will not, however, be particularly impressed if you turn shorter than anyone else and then cut in. It may be clever, but it looks a little caddish.

a 12·2 hands pony demonstrating the correct paces for the show ring: canter . . .

It is not every show, of course, that is affiliated
to the British Show Pony Society, but the majority are nowadays – and the others should be! –
and those that are have to observe very strictly
the rules about galloping. The 12·2 hands classes,
are not allowed to gallop at all, either in their
own class or even in the championship: only
individually, if the judges require them to. The
13·2 and 14·2 classes may be asked to gallop, but
never as a full class; only singly or as a group
of not more than four at the judge's discretion.

*a 14·2 hands pony
demonstrating the
correct paces for the
show ring: canter . . .*

The gallop   The 12.2 ponies are, in fact, seldom asked to gallop – only if a judge is having real difficulty in making up his mind over the first three or four.

These are excellent rules and are made entirely for the safety of the young riders.

So however tempting it may be, never send your pony into a gallop without being specifically told to do so by the judges or a steward.

The line-up   After cantering round two or three times the steward will tell you to walk, and the class will be called into a small circle to walk round the judges, who will then call in the ponies in the order they want them.

Keep an eye on the judges all the time; make sure that your pony is in their sight; in other words, don't get tucked away behind others. You can easily miss being called in, or the judges can overlook you and perhaps forget you.

If not called in do not, for goodness' sake, look disappointed or burst into tears! You can be called in quite low and go up on your show – or the badness of the displays of the others.

When called in, leave plenty of room between yourself and the pony above you, and suggest that the next pony does not come too close to you. This is bunching again; the judges want to be able to look at you properly.

Individual show   If you are somewhere near the top of the class, you will be asked to give an individual show in front of the judges. This is, perhaps, the most important part of the whole class. You should, of course, have worked out at home just what you

line-up of ponies at the South of England Show

are going to do – and *practised*; but each show ring is different, so you will now have to make up your mind quickly just where and how you are going to fit your show in.

There is one golden rule. Keep your show simple. It is much better to prepare a simple show which you can do in a faultless manner, than to be over-ambitious and come to grief.

Remember that in a child's pony the judges will first and foremost be looking for *manners* – or they should be! So attempt nothing that is going to hot your pony up and start a battle between him and you.

All the judges really want to see is the walk, trot, canter on both reins with a simple change (at the trot), a strong canter and a short gallop so that they can tell whether or not you are in complete control and can stop when required. Lastly, perhaps, they want to see a neat rein-back.

Do the whole show more or less in front of the judges where they can see you; not right away at the end of the ring, or behind a fence.

Be careful not to give yourself sharp corners to get round: you are merely making it harder for yourself than is necessary. It is much easier for you and for your pony if you take big, sweeping turns.

Make sure that your circle or your figure of eight is a good round shape. It is really very easy to do, but so often people do not do it properly. Your change of leg should come in the *centre* of the figure of eight. The more accurate your show the more your judges will be impressed.

Never look down when changing leg, as it appears very amateurish. Try as soon as possible to learn the feel: it is quite easy.

If you attempt to rein-back it is better to do it sideways on to the judges. Then if you do go crooked it is not so easy for them to notice.

Never give too long a show. It is so much better to finish before being told to stop by the judges.

On completing your show, it always looks well to drop your reins (and if you are a boy to take your cap off) and to give your pony a pat.

stripping and standing out before the judges – correct stance of pony and rider

This shows that your pony will stand still if you want it to. If there is any doubt about this, do not attempt it. If your pony will not stand, it is a bad mark for you with the judges. If the judges do not know definitely whether he stands or not, they may give him the benefit of the doubt.

Stripping and running up

When all the ponies have given their show, the judges will ask to see them stripped. Be ready for your turn, so as soon as you have finished your show have your saddle off and rub away any sweat marks. Take the reins over the pony's head and wait.

You should have learnt at home how to make your pony stand out well. If he is properly balanced on *all four legs* with his head up, he will look twice as good as when he is drooping, resting one leg or standing with his hind-legs right under him. Always stand him sideways on to the ringside, so that the spectators can have a look at him too, and stand in front of his head yourself. It is a good idea to pluck a piece of grass which he can nibble at to keep him interested and steady, and by manipulation of which you can keep his head up and his neck extended.

The judges will ask you to walk away some fifteen yards, turn and trot back. This is where a pony that leads well will gain. Handling carefully at home will have taught him to lead well Nothing looks worse than a pony being tugged while a steward chases behind.

When you turn, turn your pony away from you, do not pull him around after you.

Rosettes

As soon as your saddle is on again and you have remounted, you will in all probability be asked to walk round in a small circle while the judges make their final conclusions.

Once again, be alert; make sure that you do not miss your call, as the steward might miss you out next time.

Obviously you will be pleased if you are brought in high, but don't look disappointed if brought in low. Just accept it. Bad behaviour of any sort in the show ring is bad sportsmanship.

When the prizewinners set off round the ring with their rosettes, it is essential that they should maintain their order of merit. The spectators can see what the order is, and it prevents any sort of racing or, worse, display of bad temper by a more lowly placed competitor. You can go round either at the canter or the trot, but it is the winner who sets the pace: the others follow.

8 From the Judge's point of view

The great majority of judges at all the hundreds
of shows up and down the country are quite
impartial. Inevitably they will occasionally
recognize a pony that they have judged before,
or know a competitor; but it is unlikely that
they will be biased by this. There are other things
that are much more likely to bias them, and these
are things that are under the rider's control.

It is something that stands out that will
catch the judge's eye. It can, of course, be an
exceptionally nice-looking pony itself, but it can
be something quite small.

As soon as the class is announced, the judge
will wait and watch for the first pony to come

past him. It has gone in a flash, followed by another and another. His eye and his mind must work very fast.

Suddenly one pony will catch his eye particularly : a lovely high head carriage, perhaps, or a particularly attractive colour, or it may be the smartness of the turn-out. Or it may be that his eye has been caught for the wrong reason : a fidgety pony, a rider who looks insecure, a dirty pony; girths too loose; twisted reins.

By the time the class has walked round him a couple of times the judge has, in all probability, obtained a fairly definite view of the standard of the class, and in a very general way graded the ponies. Six or eight perhaps, seem outstanding. Another four or five are possible. The rest – some six or eight – he feels more or less certain that he will not have to bother about. And the sad thing is that often in this six or eight is a pony that ought to be in the 'outstanding' group. Perhaps its young rider has allowed it to be ignored : getting behind another pony, letting it jog all the time instead of walking.

When the judge has had his initial look at the ponies, he will ask his steward to tell them to trot. This is the time that it is very important for the young rider to keep alert. A judge does not like it if he wants to see the ponies trotting and one or two keep on walking. It gets the class in a muddle and it prevents him seeing clearly.

It is at the *trot* that one can really tell whether a horse or pony *moves*. A bad shoulder in a pony can be disguised at the walk, and up to a point at the canter, but *never* at the trot. But a bad trot can sometimes make a pony look as though it has a bad shoulder when it has not.

So with an eagle eye the judge watches the ponies trot past him. See that yours is going really well. Naturally he will look particularly at his top group. One or two will, to his disappointment, move less well than he had hoped. One of the 'possibles', on the other hand, may move really well, and the judge makes a mental note to move him up. Just possibly one of the unconsidered bunch will catch his eye.

It may seem that the judge or judges keep the class trotting rather a long time, but it is only because this is the pace which really shows him his best ponies. It shows him, too, which are the better riders, and if he sees a child, nicely turned out and riding really well, he cannot help being a little influenced.

Cantering, of course, is the most fun in the show ring, and it is a little disappointing when the judge appears to want very little cantering. But there is not all that much more he can learn from the canter; and there is still a lot to be got through before he finishes judging.

By now his mind is fairly clear. Probably he has even decided on the exact order of the first two or three. But he asks them to walk round, so that he can have a further look and make sure that he does not leave anyone out.

It may be that when he gets down to the fourth and fifth he has a little difficulty. The grey pony moved best at the trot, but has an ugly neck. The chestnut pony had a lovely head carriage; and that dun pony – a little stuffy, but a nice, genuine, typical *child's* pony.

He glances up at the rider. 'Oh dear! What a muddle. Hat on back of head with a strap under the chin; dirty jodhpurs; and the stick held like a fishing-rod. What about the one behind? Bright bay, very elegant, showy; but rather "on the leg", surely; and very short of bone and yet – the rider looks a picture: neat, efficient, a good seat, hands quiet and low. Mm, I think perhaps we'll call in the bay. The child on the dun is very much a beginner. She won't be surprised if left right out at the bottom; whereas the girl on the bay oozes experience.'

Now it may well be that the judge will later change his mind. But judges are human; they are bound to be a little bit influenced, even if subconsciously. The experienced girl cannot help suggesting a more valuable pony, even if it is in some ways easier to fault. The girl with the dirty, sloppy pony has only herself to blame if she goes down.

It is only too true, of course, that the judge is there to judge the pony, not the rider; but it is equally true that when in doubt judges will lean towards the smarter, more efficient combination.

Next the show. All the judge wants is an opportunity for a further look at the ponies, an opportunity to assess the pony's manners, its suitability for a child, and its ability to carry out a very simple test on its own. Waste no time. Be ready and as soon as it is your turn, go ahead. Above all, keep your show short.

Watching the individual show, the judge will

be comparing mentally each pony with the one before and the one after. This is his chance to reassess his order. A mistake in your show or a general muddle and the verdict is: 'A nice pony, but his show was disappointing.'

In judging children's ponies, stripping out is often a mere formality, though a judge does sometimes discover that without its saddle a pony discloses a bad shoulder or a long back. But for the most part a judge uses the stripping out just to confirm his decision.

In any case, be ready. Judges get very cross if a child is not ready, while his steward is constantly telling him that his time is running out. A really alert child will please the judge all the time. A child in a dream merely irritates him.

Judges very much enjoy the honour and privilege of judging children's ponies. Obviously they cannot please everybody, but they are not intentionally unkind. Often they make mistakes: often they appear to ignore half the class; but with classes as big as they are today, that is almost inevitable. The essential thing is to be one of the class that *does* catch the judge's eye. And it is obvious that he will prefer the pony that is well turned out, properly schooled, beautifully groomed, moves well, behaves nicely: that is ridden by a boy or girl who is smart in appearance, who obviously has ring experience, who rides well and sensibly, who looks happy and modest. In short, it is obvious that the judge will prefer the pony and rider who appear to be following some of the hints that we have attempted to expound here.

9 After the show

When you get back in the evening, make sure
first that your *pony* is well and comfortable. He
has done his best and has earned his rest. Like
you, he will be hungry and, possibly, tired.
Make a bit of a fuss of him and he will appreci-
ate it.

Take out his plaits and damp down the curls.
Remove the bandages. (Remember, incidentally,
that it is important to take just as much trouble
about the return journey, as far as your pony is
concerned, as it is about going to a show.
Don't feel that because the show is over nothing
matters. Accidents can happen just as easily on
the way home, or even unboxing at home.)
Brush all the sweat off and in a general way
freshen him up. If you are going to turn your
pony out, give him a feed first. It will be a little
treat for him and more interesting than the
usual grass in his own field.

When you are satisfied that everything has
been done for your pony, then you can retire
yourself. It may not be easy to sit down and eat
a proper meal, let alone go to bed; you will still
be excited; there will still be so much to talk
about. What fun it is, always, lingering over
all the incidents and excitements of the day.
But whatever you do, resist the temptation of
running down the judging and criticizing those
who may have beaten you. Quite possibly the
judges make mistakes: they are only human

and, anyway, it is a matter of opinion. You may feel that your pony was better than the pony in front of you. But it could be that on this particular occasion you did not show it so well. Even if it does genuinely seem that you were unlucky, well, take it all in good part. Don't be too serious about it, as you will take all the fun out of showing. The knowledge that you have done your best for yourself and for your pony is the real reward.

Good luck, then, and may your saddle-room, bed-room, sitting-room or kitchen be full of rosettes!

Index